CLIMBING THE LADDER ON TROCHAIC FEET

**POETIC REFLECTIONS ON
THE LADDER OF DIVINE ASCENT
— STEPS 1 & 2 —**

KENNETH A. O'SHAUGHNESSY

O'Shaughnessy Publications
Simpsonville, South Carolina

Published by O'Shaughnessy Publications
501 Agewood Drive
Simpsonville, South Carolina 29680

www.kempisosha.com

© 2017 by O'Shaughnessy Publications

Library of Congress Control Number: 2013916625

International Standard Book No: 978-0-615-95469-1

All images within the book are clipped from the public domain image of the icon of the Divine Ladder of Ascent shown in part on the title page.

All rights reserved

PRINTED IN THE UNITED STATES OF AMERICA

Climbing The Ladder On Trochaic Feet

For:

All
Laddering
Disciples

Climbing The Ladder On Trochaic Feet
APOPHATIC APOLOGY

You already know what a blog is.
You're looking at it.
You know what poetry is,
at least when you see it.
You can use Wikipedia to find out
what The Ladder of Divine Ascent is
and you can read it on or offline.
But neither you nor the interweb
know what this project will be,
nor even yet do I.
But I can tell you what
the project will not be.
The project won't be quick.
I found a lenten lectionary
which I won't be following
but which indicates it won't
take much less than a year
at the very minimum.
The project won't be expository.
The project won't be translation of
the text into poetic formulae.
The project won't be for everybody.
The project won't be babies and butterflies.
The project will not be televised,
will not be televised,
will not be televised.
The project will be no re-run, brothers.
The project will be...

The project will be trochaic.
A trochaic foot looks like this:
[' /u]
One step up, one step down
much like I expect this climb
up the Ladder will be.
I just hope I don't walk
on dactyl feet -
One step forward, two steps back.

Continued

Climbing The Ladder On Trochaic Feet

What's the reason, you ask?
What's the reason you ask?
That's what I'm doing, is asking.
If you want questions, keep reading.
If you want answers, pray.
If you've got answers, keep quiet.
Only questioners talk too much.
People with answers stay busy
listening -
The silence of Job, when his friends
were giving him the answers
to the wrong questions,
when God was giving him the questions
to the answers he already had.

The project will not be silent
until the last question mark is dotted
by the finger of God.

~~~~~~~~

The text of *The Divine Ladder of Ascent* by St John Climacus is presented here as translated by Archimandrite Lazarus Moore and found online at http://www.prudencetrue.com/images/TheLadderofDivineAscent.pdf

My musings were initially posted on and further posts can be read at http://trochaicfeet.blogspot.com/

Once we begin our progress up the Ladder, each spread will present a numbered passage from *The Divine Ladder* on the left, and my poetry inspired by the section on the right.

Climbing The Ladder On Trochaic Feet
Preparing to Climb

Sycamore

You can't see God and you can't see man
You've got to get above them any way you can
When you come up a little short find a way to leave
Grow up in a sycamore and you'll believe

See the Savior passing by
Hear him stop and ask you why
You climbed up when you can fly
All you have to do is die

Lay your head on the stone that breaks your heart
Got to prostrate on the ground to make your start
Sleeping in the house of God will make you dream
Of a ladder up to Heaven where you'll come clean

See the Savior passing by
Hear him stop and ask you why
You climbed up when you can fly
All you have to do is die

If you wanna climb the ladder you've got to see
First you've gotta climb the sycamore tree
You've gotta see the Word before the climb
He's gotta measure every foot of every rhyme

See the Savior passing by
Hear him stop and ask you why
You climbed up when you can fly
All you have to do is die

Climbing The Ladder On Trochaic Feet

Preparing to Climb

How does one begin to climb a ladder?

How does one begin to climb a ladder?
One does not simply start stepping skyward
Sight unseen
If one wants to be sure of safely touching the sky
Or the ground

There are things we think about
Without thinking about them
Does the ladder touch the sky?
Does the ladder reach the ground?
Is there a beginning and a destiny?
Is there a ladder where you are?
Is there a ladder?

Everything comes down to us
It starts from above and comes down
Like the little ladder leading into the attic
But life-long
But, interestingly,
Angels ascend before decending
Showing us the way to go, and how
They empty themselves of angel-ness
And hold on like a human
Clawing out of primordial soup
And into the image of God

Have I mentioned yet I hate heights?
Not in the "It's not the fall that bothers me,
It's the sudden stop at then end" sense
But in the "If there was a rational reason
I wouldn't be scared anymore" sense
I happen to like where I am
Down here

Continued

Climbing The Ladder On Trochaic Feet

But this isn't where we were made for
Otherwise we'd have stayed in the soup
A bottomed-out we can't remember
And just like we are bottomless
We must try to go topless also
And so we must begin the climb by being
Naked and ashamed until we are
Covered in that which we stole
Legless like the serpent
Raised to walk in newness of life
With knees that we know will bend

When you climb a ladder you won't
Look back and see footprints in the sand
You'll just see the solid ground
Such a long distance and short time away
But you don't have to worry about falling
You will fall; you just don't have to worry
You will start climbing again and again
The ladder doesn't seem solid
Until you are broken

Preparing to Climb

Isn't This Book for Monastics?

If you know anything about the Ladder
You may be wanting to ask:
Isn't this book for monastics?
Aren't you a married man?
Ponder what St Paul said in the Church yesterday:
"Let those who have wives live as though they had none"
If I am living that way
It isn't in obedience to that injunction
Because monastacism is obedience
Placing yourself beneath another
So you can be lifted up.
I have not yet developed the weakness
Necessary to bearing another's burden:
Knees so weak I have to bow
Hands so weak I have to let go
Voice so weak I have to listen
Eyes so weak I have to be led
Will so weak I have to be obedient
Heart so weak I have to be given life.
For when I am weak
Then am I free.
Think you're strong enough to make the climb?
Belay that thought!
Even the monastics don't go it on their own
Until they are broken
And even then only under obedience.
And even then they have the wild beasts
And the wilder spirits of God
To bear them up when they fall.

Monastics are simply siblings
Sons and daughters of the same Father
And this book is a series of letters
From a Father to his children
It's a long and glorious tradition
Begun by the Father of us all

Continued

Climbing The Ladder On Trochaic Feet

Is the Torah for goyim?
Hibernian as I may be
And lost as any lost tribe of Israel
The Torah teaches me, too
That law is something to love
That God is the Lord
And has revealed Himself to us
That obedience is the only freedom
That I am His son,
This day has He begotten me

I've never known my father very well
I'm the spoiled rich boy
Who blames his behavior on his dad
Who provides him with everything
And acts like gifts aren't part of dear old dad
Gifts aren't from the heart
They are the heart
And the mind
And the soul
Any time you give you give yourself
Anything you're given is someone else
If you want to know God
Use what you're given

This book is a gift
And I haven't yet used it
All gifts have to be bought
By both giver and receiver
And it's time for me to buy in

ON RENUNCIATION OF THE WORLD

1

Our God and King is good, ultra-good and all-good (it is best to begin with God in writing to the servants of God). Of the rational beings created by Him and honoured with the dignity of free-will, some are His friends, others are His true servants, some are worthless, some are completely estranged from God, and others, though feeble creatures are equally His opponents. By friends of God, dear and holy Father, we simple people mean, properly speaking, those intellectual and incorporeal beings which surround God. By true servants of God we mean all those who tirelessly and unremittingly do and have done His will. By worthless servants we mean those who think of themselves as having been granted baptism, but have not faithfully kept the vows they made to God. By those estranged from God and alienated from Him, we mean those who are unbelievers or heretics. Finally, the enemies of God are those who have not only evaded and rejected the Lord's commandment themselves, but who also wage bitter war on those who are fulfilling it.

On Trochaic Feet
GOOD GOD! WHAT A DREAM!

Good God! What a dream!
Comes from pillowing on a rock, I suppose,
Like an offering laid out on an altar;
Which comes from sleeping in the House of God;
Which comes from leaving the world behind.
Let me tell you my dream, my brothers,
My mothers and my father- no sheaves or stars,
This time it's the real and good King-
Apparently the Temple of Creation has an attic.
Somebody drops the divine ladder down,
And a mass movement begins,
Descending, ascending, descending, ascending.
You'd expect some boxes, or antique furniture,
But nobody's carrying anything.
It's quite a cast of characters, apparently
Representing all sentient beings;
I, in my semi-sentient watching state,
Am safer on the stone pillow awaiting sacrifice.
At the top, among the popcorn-ceiling clouds,
God's fine-feathered friends assist the faithful,
Who climb hand-over-hand, rung after rung,
Eyes fixed on the attic-dweller.
Below them, sometimes above them,
But always going back downward,
Are those clambering like children
Monkeying on a jungle gym.
They've passed the playground initiation,
But they think that being children is child's play.
Going up and growing up:
Both of them require heads in the clouds.
Near the foot you find some sitting,
Like a child on the stoop afraid
To go in and face his father.
At the base there are the ladder-deniers.
They may deny just the attic or attic-dweller
But believe the ladder is good exercise.
They may believe man crawled up just this far
And just this far is the top, nowhere left to go
Except the tiny vastness of vacuum.
They dig down deep to discern the denouement
Instead of looking up, and end up
Hollowing out their own Hades.
I think there were a couple kinds of people
Left off the ladder's line-up:
Those hounded off by heretics or demons-
If there's any actual difference-
Who, I think, tend to fall up;
And sleepers like me.

ON RENUNCIATION OF THE WORLD

2

*E*ach of the classes mentioned above might well have a special treatise devoted to it. But for simple folk like us it would not be profitable at this point to enter into such lengthy investigations. Come then, in unquestioning obedience let us stretch out our unworthy hand to the true servants of God who devoutly compel us and in their faith constrain us by their commands. Let us write this treatise with a pen taken from their knowledge and dipped in the ink of humility which is both subdued yet radiant. Then let us apply it to the smooth white paper of their hearts, or rather rest it on the tablets of the spirit, and let us inscribe the divine words (or rather sow the seeds). And let us begin like this.

On Trochaic Feet
HUMBLE PIE IN THE SKY

Let's begin
On the ground
On our face
With no sound

Lift our face
To the sky
Wait for the
Humble pie

All we really need to know is look
And all we need to do is listen
Make our paper hearts an open book
Watch the stars above us glisten

Watch the true
As they climb
Still as death
Take your time

Put to death
Other thoughts
No need to
Cast the lots

All we really need to know is look
And all we need to do is listen
Make our paper hearts an open book
Watch the stars above us glisten

Let us raise our hands to those above
And let the stars of Heaven guide us
Make our paper hearts a book of love
And climb the ladder that's inside us

Let's begin
On the ground
On our face
With no sound

Lift our face
To the sky
Wait for the
Humble pie

ON RENUNCIATION OF THE WORLD

3

God belongs to all free beings. He is the life of all, the salvation of all—faithful and unfaithful, just and unjust, pious and impious, passionate and dispassionate, monks and seculars, wise and simple, healthy and sick, young and old—just as the diffusion of light, the sight of the sun, and the changes of the weather are for all alike; 'for there is no respect of persons with God'.

On Trochaic Feet
GO ON AND GRAB A SUNBEAM

Go on and grab a sunbeam
It's all yours if you can
You can catch it with your eyeballs
Your open mouth or hand
Go on and grab a sunbeam
Illuminate your life
It's the light that lights the way of every man

If you are good or evil
Or a mixture of the two
If you are kind of foolish
Or an incredible IQ
If you are hot as Hades
Or cold as the ninth ring down
If you're in love with God above
Or believe that He's a clown

Go on and grab a sunbeam
It's all yours if you can
You can catch it with your eyeballs
Your open mouth or hand
Go on and grab a sunbeam
Illuminate your life
It's the light that lights the way of every man

And when the skies are open
And rain is pouring down
You can use that sunbeam
To drive away your frown
A smile's the best umbrella
That's what they always say
And all the while you'll have a smile
If you're carrying the day

Go on and grab a sunbeam
It's all yours if you can
You can catch it with your eyeballs
Your open mouth or hand
Go on and grab a sunbeam
Illuminate your life
It's the light that lights the way of every man

Continued

Climbing The Ladder

Step 1 Page 20

On Trochaic Feet

One thing you can be sure of
If a sunbeam you do get
How it will affect you
Is what you do with it
Be grateful that you've got one
And everything is swell
Try to hide it and you'll find it
Can really burn like Hell

So go on and grab a sunbeam
It's all yours if you can
You can catch it with your eyeballs
Your open mouth or hand
Go on and grab a sunbeam
Illuminate your life
It's the light that lights the way of every man

ON RENUNCIATION OF THE WORLD

4

The irreligious man is a mortal being with a rational nature, who of his own free will turns his back on life and thinks of his own Maker, the ever-existent, as non-existent. The lawless man is one who holds the law of God after his own depraved fashion, and thinks to combine faith in God with heresy that is directly opposed to Him. The Christian is one who imitates Christ in thought, word and deed, as far as is possible for human beings, believing rightly and blamelessly in the Holy Trinity. The lover of God is he who lives in communion with all that is natural and sinless, and as far as he is able neglects nothing good. The continent man is he who in the midst of temptations, snares and turmoil, strives with all his might to imitate the ways of Him who is free from such. The monk is he who within his earthly and soiled body toils towards the rank and state of the incorporeal beings. A monk is he who strictly controls his nature and unceasingly watches over his senses. A monk is he who keeps his body in chastity, his mouth pure and his mind illumined. A monk is a mourning soul that both asleep and awake is unceasingly occupied with the remembrance of death. Withdrawal from the world is voluntary hatred of vaunted material things and denial of nature for the attainment of what is above nature.

On Trochaic Feet
THE BALLAD OF THE MONASTERY

~ To the tune of "The Ballad of Gilligan's Isle"

Just sit right back and you'll hear a hymn
A hymn that's out of this world
Of a ship that's headed Heavenward
As from this Earth it's hurled
We've all got to find a way to sail
on the sea of eternity
Best ship off the ground as you're Heaven-bound
Is the Monastery
The Monastery

The Monastery ships all kinds, it's a microcosmic earth
Let's look over the passenger list and see who's taken berth
And see who's taken berth

The ship set forth Heavenward on the sea of eternity
With the Atheist
And the Heretic
The Troubador, and his wife
The Christian
The Confessor and the Brotherhood
Here in the Monastery

So here is the tale of our sailing crew
And their vaporous sunburnt trip
And the lessons we learn for our own sail
On our terrestrial ship

Remember the One Who walked the sea
Walk the waves with eyes on Him
Remember death comes all too soon
Keep your mind and body trim

Stay away from port til you reach that rest
'Til the ship grounds on the mount
Shake the earth from off your feet
And make every last step count

So join the Brothers as they sail
To that kingdom 'cross the sea
Wave as you leave the world behind
In the Monastery

ON RENUNCIATION OF THE WORLD

5

All who have willingly left the things of the world, have certainly done so either for the sake of the future Kingdom, or because of the multitude of their sins, or for love of God. If they were not moved by any of these reasons their withdrawal from the world was unreasonable. But God who sets our contests waits to see what the end of our course will be.

On Trochaic Feet
GET AWAY!

Get away! Go to Kingdom Come
Face it man - this old world is not your home
There's a mansion in the sky
In the sweet sweet by and by
Where you will never ever cry
And nowhere lost to roam

Get away! You're a sinful man
With your sin, you brought a curse on the land
Thorns and thistles choke your life
Work and sorrow, pain and strife
Saved by child-bearing wife
And hammer in your hand

Get away, for the love of God!
All too soon you will rest beneath the sod
Work and only stop to pray
Always mournful, never gay
Walk with death in your way
Be raised up by the rod

Get away! Do not go and rest
Do not play - Damnation is not a jest
If you want to rule the world
Keep the riches that you've squirreled
Into Hell you will be hurled
And that is for your best

Climbing The Ladder

On Trochaic Feet
SIMON SAYS

Simon says:
Leave the world
Bring in the kingdom by force
Drag them kicking and screaming
Better to be kicking and screaming and living
Than to be kicking and screaming and burning
Manhandle them with mercy

Simon says:
Leave the world
Thou art the Christ, I don't know you
It is good for us to be here
So you could restore the servant's severed ear
With my mouth I bless and curse and swear
Go out and cry bitterly

Simon says:
Leave the world
You know three times I love you, Lord
I went fishing and left the nets
Jumped in and never hedged my bets
I'll be crucified with no regrets
Called to virtue and glory

Leave the world
Purchase the power of God
Lay on hands in Jesus' name
Speak the Word and feel no shame
Gather riches and power and fame
I did not say Simon says...

ON RENUNCIATION OF THE WORLD

6

The man who has withdrawn from the world in order to shake off his own burden of sins, should imitate those who sit outside the city amongst the tombs, and should not discontinue his hot and fiery streams of tears and voiceless heartfelt groanings until he, too, sees that Jesus has come to him and rolled away the stone of hardness from his heart, and loosed Lazarus, that is to say, our mind, from the bands of sin, and ordered His attendant angels: Loose him from passions, and let him go to blessed dispassion. Otherwise he will have gained nothing.

On Trochaic Feet
AND I CRY

Go down among the empty tombs
Full of bones and dust and dank
That's where I'm bound with broken chains
Full of groans and lust and stank
Hear the songs I scream at night
The art I cut into my flesh
High on the hog society
Where the blood is always fresh

And I cry
And I cry
And I cry
Lord, have mercy on me

One day a man who opens graves
And by death he conquers Death
Came to my cemetery plot
And his breath became my breath
He spoke the words that forged my chains
And he fettered me to him
Then left me with a mournful joy
And a celebration grim

And I cry
And I cry
And I cry
Lord, have mercy on me

And now I sit among the tombs
All is silent but the cry
Of one who's waiting for a Savior
To once again pass by
Let me tell you of the death
I never have to die again
And the death I choose to live
Until I am free from sin

And I cry
And I cry
And I cry
Lord, have mercy on me

ON RENUNCIATION OF THE WORLD

7

Those of us who wish to go out of Egypt and to fly from Pharaoh, certainly need some Moses as a mediator with God and from God, who, standing between action and contemplation, will raise hands of prayer for us to God, so that guided by Him we may cross the sea of sin and rout the Amalek of the passions. That is why those who have surrendered themselves to God, deceive themselves if they suppose that they have no need of a director. Those who came out of Egypt had Moses as their guide, and those who fled from Sodom had an angel. The former are like those who are healed of the passions of the soul by the care of physicians: these are they who come out of Egypt. The latter are like those who long to put off the uncleanness of the wretched body. That is why they need a helper, an angel, so to speak, or at least one equal to an angel. For in proportion to the corruption of our wounds we need a director who is indeed an expert and a physician.

On Trochaic Feet
I NEED AN ANGEL

I flee from fondled bondage
To a reptilian king
To worship the Creator
Instead of everything
I run into the river
That boils me in cold blood
An angel sent from Heaven
Takes me through the flood

Oh God I need an angel
I can't escape the flame
The passion burns within me
My face burns with the shame
And oh God I need an angel
To keep me from the fall
Oh God I need an angel
To God damn them all

I wander in the desert
I burn with thirst and dust
I'm lost and I am lonely
Full of hunger and of lust
If I could find my own way
I'd die here in the heat
An angel sent from Heaven
Gives me God as drink and meat

Oh God I need an angel
I can't escape the flame
The passion burns within me
My face burns with the shame
And oh God I need an angel
To keep me from the fall
Oh God I need an angel
To God damn them all

Continued

Climbing The Ladder

On Trochaic Feet

I dwell here in this city
Of forgotten deities
Betrayed by the fifth column
And beaten to my knees
Oh God I need an angel
I've no strength to hold this sword
Oh God please send an angel
The Angel of the Lord

Oh God I need an angel
I can't escape the flame
The passion burns within me
My face burns with the shame
And oh God I need an angel
To keep me from the fall
Oh God I need an angel
To God damn them all

ON RENUNCIATION OF THE WORLD

8

Those who aim at ascending with the body to heaven, need violence indeed and constant suffering especially in the early stages of their renunciation, until our pleasure-loving dispositions and unfeeling hearts attain to love of God and chastity by visible sorrow. A great toil, very great indeed, with much unseen suffering, especially for those who live carelessly, until by simplicity, deep angerlessness and diligence, we make our mind, which is a greedy kitchen dog addicted to barking, a lover of chastity and watchfulness. But let us who are weak and passionate have the courage to offer our infirmity and natural weakness to Christ with unhesitating faith, and confess it to Him; and we shall be certain to obtain His help, even beyond our merit, if only we unceasingly go right down to the depth of humility.

On Trochaic Feet
BEAT DOWN

Gotta be beat down, beat down
If you want a heavenly body
Beat down, beat down
If you wanna be whole
You gotta be beat down, beat down
And you've got to enjoy it
Beat down, beat down
Deep within your soul

Like a greedy dog 'neath the kitchen table
Running around licking every hand
My mind is in every way unstable
It won't sit still, play dead or stand
There's only one fix for this situation
It'll hurt bad but it's gotta be done
Gotta beat him to humiliation
Or else I'm gonna have to get the gun

Gotta be beat down, beat down
If you want a heavenly body
Beat down, beat down
If you wanna be whole
You gotta be beat down, beat down
And you've got to enjoy it
Beat down, beat down
Deep within your soul

I'm used to watching his hand for favors
Begging for him to throw me a bone
I've just got to learn some new behaviors
Shut my yap and change my tone
My job is to watch the doors and windows
Keep the place safe from the thief in the night
Instead I'm always barking at shadows
And I am all bark and no bite

Continued

Climbing The Ladder

On Trochaic Feet

Gotta be beat down, beat down
If you want a heavenly body
Beat down, beat down
If you wanna be whole
You gotta be beat down, beat down
And you've got to enjoy it
Beat down, beat down
Deep within your soul

So now I'm dancing the belly shuffle
Nose to the ground, ears drag on the floor
Learning to love the sound of silence
Waiting for a Good Boy once more
And if I ever get distracted
Greedy or angry or simply bored
I hope my master will get the switch out
Remind me who is dog and who's lord

Gotta be beat down, beat down
If you want a heavenly body
Beat down, beat down
If you wanna be whole
You gotta be beat down, beat down
And you've got to enjoy it
Beat down, beat down
Deep within your soul

On Renunciation of the World

9

*A*ll who enter upon the good fight, which is hard and narrow, but also easy, must realize that they must leap into the fire, if they really expect the celestial fire to dwell in them. But, let everyone examine himself, and so let him eat the bread of it with its bitter herbs, and let him drink the cup of it with its tears, lest his service lead to his own judgment. If everyone who has been baptized has not been saved—I shall be silent about what follows.[1]

1 This means: 'If every baptized person is not saved, so the same can be said about monks—not all who have made the vow are real monks and will be saved. But I prefer to pass over this matter in silence.'

On Trochaic Feet
BURN LIKE A MARTYR

You've got to burn like a martyr
If you want the fire inside
You can only have the vision
In eyes that have cried
You can only fill the hunger
With bitter herbs and bread
You are only truly living
When you are truly dead
So go down into the river
Where the holy water burns
Come out with your soul on fire
And live the life a martyr earns

If you want to be a brother
Better look before you leap
Got to eat herbs of forgiveness
Got to cry instead of sleep
Got to burn with that desire
That makes martyrs of us all
If you want to save your own life
Then you've got to save them all
So bow down before your brother
And take from him his load
If you only carry yourself
Better to not go down that road

If you want to be a warrior
Win the battle and the day
You've got to charge into the fire
Down the hard and narrow way
And then you'll find it's easy
Your tears keep your eyes clear
Your hunger keeps you going
And death takes away your fear
So come and be my brother
Come and fight by my side
You've got to burn like a martyr
If you want the fire inside

ON RENUNCIATION OF THE WORLD

10

Those who enter this contest must renounce all things, despise all things, deride all things, and shake off all things, that they may lay a firm foundation. A good foundation of three layers and three pillars is innocence, fasting and temperance. Let all babes in Christ begin with these virtues, taking as their model the natural babes. For you never find in them anything sly or deceitful. They have no insatiate appetite, no insatiable stomach, no body on fire; but perhaps as they grow, in proportion as they take more food, their natural passions also increase.

On Trochaic Feet
LET'S GO OUT

Let's go out and see the world baby
See it from the outside in
'Cause you got those innocent eyes baby
You don't even know how to sin
The road is open so let's go baby
We got some wheels and godspeed
Leave this boring life behind you, baby
There ain't all that much you need

Let's go out and fill our bellies baby
With the mother's milk of love
And we'll share the rest with others baby
A little bit is more than enough
The road is open so let's go baby
We got some wheels and godspeed
Leave this empty life behind you, baby
There ain't all that much you need

Let's go out and find our happy baby
No matter what comes our way
Peaceful from the inside outside baby
We only keep what we give away
The road is open so let's go baby
We got some wheels and godspeed
Leave this busy life behind you, baby
There ain't all that much you need

Let's go out until we get home baby
Won't be 'til the dark of the dawn
Fill our tank up with the spirit baby
We'll drive until the gasoline's gone
The road is open so let's go baby
We got some wheels and godspeed
Leave this grown-up life behind you, baby
There ain't all that much you need

ON RENUNCIATION OF THE WORLD

11

To lag in the fight at the very outset of the struggle and thereby to furnish proof of our coming defeat is a very hateful and dangerous thing. A firm beginning will certainly be useful for us when we later grow slack. A soul that is strong at first but then relaxes is spurred on by the memory of its former zeal. And in this way new wings are often obtained.

On Trochaic Feet
FLAP LIKE A FOOL

I'm the baby bird that never flew
Who never had the strength in his wings
I am the angel who never fell
But for whom the bell never rings

But I'd flap like a fool if I was pushed from the nest
And if Heaven opened up, I'd pray to be blessed
And once I was flying, I'd never rest

I'm the butterfly who never left the cocoon
For whom the freeze just came too soon
I am the aircraft only in plans
Never shot for the sky, only the moon

But I'd flap like a fool if I could unfold my wings
And if Heaven opened up, the sound barrier would sing
And once I was flying, you'd see some things

I'm the bumblebee too heavy to fly
Kept up by God and miracle wings
I am the soul unbound from the Earth
Sent up to Heaven on eternal hope springs

But I'd flap like a fool if it weren't for angel wings
And if Heaven opened up, the angel choir would sing
And once I was flying, I'd be borne to the King

ON RENUNCIATION OF THE WORLD

12

When the soul betrays itself and loses the blessed and longed for fervour, let it carefully investigate the reason for losing this. And let it arm itself with all its longing and zeal against whatever has caused this. For the former fervour can return only through the same door through which it was lost.

On Trochaic Feet
WHEN YOU'VE LOST

When you've lost your way
How you gonna get home
No words to pray
How you gonna save your soul
Gotta know where you are lost
Before you can be found
Remember where you turned around

When you've lost your mind
What are you thinking
No words to pray
How you gonna save your soul
It's only when you know you're sick
That you can be made whole
Remember where you lost control

When you've lost your love
How are you living
No words to pray
How you gonna save your soul
All that you can do is serve
Until love comes to stay
Remember where you lost your way

On Renunciation of the World

13

The man who renounces the world from fear is like burning incense, that begins with fragrance but ends in smoke. He who leaves the world through hope of reward is like a millstone, that always moves in the same way. But he who withdraws from the world out of love for God has obtained fire at the very outset; and, like fire set to fuel, it soon kindles a larger fire.

On Trochaic Feet
RUNNING

Running away
I have to leave the world behind
But I keep looking over my shoulder
And it's myself I find
I can't leave the world
Because it is in my mind

Running around
I have to leave this worldly care
But it's me that has gone through the mill
I can't get anywhere
I'm ground into the world
I just want to win my share

Running toward
The one who is my eternal reward
Doesn't matter what I've left behind
Except the fiery sward
I am dead to the world
For I'm alive in the Lord

ON RENUNCIATION OF THE WORLD

14

Some build bricks upon stones. Others set pillars on the bare ground. And there are some who go a short distance and, having got their muscles and joints warm, go faster. Whoever can understand, let him understand this allegorical word.

On Trochaic Feet
THE WAY TO HOLINESS

Once upon a time, there were three little meerkats. Why meerkats, you ask? Because they are cute, they do that standing up and looking thing, and they live in the desert like monks. Anyway, these three little meerkats were trying to live lives of ascetical virtue and obtain mercy for their souls. What? Of course that's what meerkats do - why else would they live in the desert in communities?

As it happens in all monastic communities, a dispute arose between the three meerkats about the best way to strive for holiness. Together they went to the Hieromeerkat Timon to ask for permission to test their theological theories. Brother Wynken believed hard work was the best way to godliness. Brother Blynken insisted it was strict asceticism. And Brother Nod believed that getting away from the cares of this life would bring him nearest to God.

"Abba Timon," they said to him, bowing low, "We beg your leave to each enter the desert and live each according to his way, to determine which is the best path to holiness." They remained on the floor of Hieromeerkat Timon's cave awaiting his answer.

"Brothers Wynken, Blynken and Nod, please raise yourselves up," Hieromeerkat Timon told them. "You should try to work things out in the monastery." In one accord, the Brothers began to argue with their abbot. He sighed. "If you are going to argue anyway, please do so in the desert." And he dismissed them.

The Brothers gathered their things for their foray into the desert. Brother Wynken took his tool bag and service book. Brother Blynken took his - well, nothing, really - strict asceticism, remember? And Brother Nod took his copy of the Philokalia.

Out in the desert they went to seek their treasures in Heaven. Brother Wynken went to a place not too close to the river where he could build himself a hut of large stones and labouriously scratch out a garden. Brother Blynken went to a flat place where he could erect a pillar, where he would spend his entire time out in the desert eating sunlight and drinking rainwater. And Brother Nod found a natural shelter near an oasis.

Continued

Climbing The Ladder

On Trochaic Feet

Brother Blynken found that he could not erect the pillar without the help of Brother Wynken's strength. Brother Nod found that the oasis was a regular stop on the trade routes and he needed Brother Blynken to let him know when he should run away into the desert to escape the worldliness. And both Brothers Wynken and Blynken found they needed Brother Nod to bring them food, at least a little, so they wouldn't starve to death.

After living in the desert this way for a few months, the brothers gathered together to discuss what they had learned. They discovered that they had come to a consensus and were ready to return to Hieromeerkat Timon to make their report.

They came before Hieromeerkat Timon and bowed low. "Abba Timon, we believe we have learned the lesson of holiness that we went into the desert to find," they told him. "We have learned that the way to holiness isn't work, asceticism, or escape form the world, but it is brotherly love." They hugged one another before the Hieromeerkat with pleased grins on their faces.

"My children," said Hieromeerkat Timon kindly, "You were all wrong before you went into the desert, and you are still all wrong." The Brothers' faces fell. "I told you you should try to work things out in the monastery, and instead you went into the desert. You went your own way. The only way to holiness is obedience."

ON RENUNCIATION OF THE WORLD

15

*L*et us eagerly run our course as men called by our God and King, lest, since our time is short, we be found in the day of our death without fruit and perish of hunger. Let us please the Lord as soldiers please their king; because we are required to give an exact account of our service after the campaign. Let us fear the Lord not less than we fear beasts. For I have seen men who were going to steal and were not afraid of God, but, hearing the barking of dogs, they at once turned back; and what the fear of God could not achieve was done by the fear of animals. Let us love God at least as much as we respect our friends. For I have often seen people who had offended God and were not in the least perturbed about it. And I have seen how those same people provoked their friends in some trifling matter and then employed every artifice, every device, every sacrifice, every apology, both personally and through friends and relatives, not sparing gifts, in order to regain their former love.

On Trochaic Feet
Of course God's watching

Of course God's watching
And I know He's waiting
And I know He's calling
My name
But I am busy
And He'll still be there
Since He is always the same

Of course God's watching
And I know He's waiting
And I know He's calling
My name
There are things I want
And no one's watching
So I can get things without shame

Of course God's watching
And I know He's waiting
And I know He's calling
My name
But there's those I love
That are mad at me
And I am the one to blame

Of course God's watching
And I know He's waiting
And I know He's calling
My name
But I am running
Away from something
And I feel hunger and flame

Of course God's watching
And I know He's waiting
And I know He's calling
My name
So I'll run to him
And beg for mercy
Forget each worldly claim

ON RENUNCIATION OF THE WORLD

16

*I*n the very beginning of our renunciation, it is certainly with labour and grief that we practise the virtues. But when we have made progress in them, we no longer feel sorrow, or we feel little sorrow. But as soon as our mortal mind is consumed, and mastered by our alacrity, we practise them with all joy and eagerness, with love and with divine fire.

On Trochaic Feet
ENJOYABLE PAIN

Push up
Pull up
Run up
Fall down

Muscles burn
Bones aching
Joints melting

Body rebels
Get up again
Push through the pain
Make a small gain
Keep up the strain

Making it farther
Feeling lighter
Anticipation
Enjoyable pain

Can't wait to go again
Going the full distance
Vaulting over the top
The adrenaline rush
And the strong beating heart

And your body filled with fire

On renunciation of the world

17

Those who at once from the very outset follow the virtues and fulfil the commandments with joy and alacrity certainly deserve praise. And in the same way those who spend a long time in asceticism[4] and still find it a weariness to obey the commandments, if they obey them at all, certainly deserve pity.

4 *This might also be translated: 'dawdle over their training'.*

On Trochaic Feet
YOU SIR

You sir are so very prompt
And joyful in your work
You have earned my meager praise
A task I will not shirk

You sir seem so very tired
And slow to get things done
You have my pity, for I'm sure
It's hard for you, my son

You sir no matter what you do
Do not deserve my curse
I've been where both of you are
And probably much worse

ON RENUNCIATION OF THE WORLD

18

Let us not even abhor or condemn the renunciation due merely to circumstances. I have seen men who had fled into exile meet the emperor by accident when he was on tour, and then join his company, enter his palace, and dine with him. I have seen seed casually fall on the earth and bear plenty of thriving fruit. And I have seen the opposite, too. I have also seen a person come to a hospital with some other motive, but the courtesy and kindness of the physician overcame him, and on being treated with an astringent, he got rid of the darkness that lay on his eyes. Thus for some the unintentional was stronger and more sure than what was intentional in others.

On Trochaic Feet
DON'T COUNT OUT

Don't count out the running man
As long as he's flying you don't know where he'll land
He may stumble and fall until he hears the call
To be the honored guest of the ruler of all

Don't count out the castaway
You don't know what might sprout by the end of the day
It just might thrive and grow and bear an hundredfold
And bear all the fruit that a seed can hold

Don't count out the cunning thief
If he's stretching the truth he may find belief
He may come in to steal and go away healed
And all he was hiding may be revealed

Don't count out the pious one
You don't know his end until his race is run
If he falls in disgrace he may still see God's face
As long as he throws himself on God's grace

ON RENUNCIATION OF THE WORLD

19

Let no one, by appealing to the weight and multitude of his sins, say that he is unworthy of the monastic vow, and for love of pleasure disparage himself, excusing himself with excuses in his sins.[1] Where there is much corruption, considerable treatment is needed to draw out all the impurity. The healthy do not go to a hospital.

1 *Psalm cxl, 4. The meaning is that in the midst of his sins he makes excuses for not becoming a monk. The excuses are not for his sins, but his sins are his excuses.*

On Trochaic Feet
VOWS

There are not very many vows in the Church
Vows are made only to God, not man
Or by God to man
Baptism is a vow of man to God
Marriage is a vow of God to man
What God has joined together
Let no man put asunder
What man has put together
Is already broken

Monastics used to become holy
Just by taking up a habit
Like we take the robe or crown
We baptise our babies
While they are without excuse
And have nothing to excuse
And they take their vows
By mouths that only eat and cry
To keep living that way
Their robes remaining unstained

By the time we can speak our vows
We've already broken them
Stained robes have become our habits
Filthy and holey but comfortable
And we don't want to change into
The hair shirt that is holy and clean
We excuse our diseases
And our diseases become our excuse
We add hypochondria
To our list of real ailments
And take a placebo for them all

So like a newborn child or bride
Become and remain chaste
By giving yourself up completely
Become and remain poor
By having nothing all your own
Become and remain obedient
By only giving and receiving
Become and remain steadfast
By making the habit your habit
By paying your vows unto the Lord
In the presence of all His people

ON RENUNCIATION OF THE WORLD

20

If an earthly king were to call us and request us to serve in his presence, we should not delay for other orders, we should not make excuses, but we should leave everything and eagerly go to him. Let us then be on the alert, lest when the King of kings and Lord of lords and God of gods calls us to this heavenly office, we cry off out of sloth and cowardice and find ourselves without excuse at the Last Judgment. It is possible to walk, even when tied with the fetters of worldly affairs and iron cares, but only with difficulty. For even those who have iron chains on their feet can often walk; but they are continually stumbling and getting hurt. An unmarried man, who is only tied to the world by business affairs, is like one who has fetters on his hands; and therefore when he wishes to enter the monastic life he has nothing to hinder him. But the married man is like one who is bound hand and foot. (So when he wants to run he cannot.)[2]

2 *The words in parenthesis are missing in some versions and may be an interpolation.*

On Trochaic Feet
BOUND

I am bound for the Promised Land
Bound hand and foot
Am I trying to get to the King,
Or just trying to get away from the Queen?
So much world, so many affairs,
So much business, so many cares.
There's role-mandated frolicking,
There's prayers we wish we'd done,
There's arguments and laughter,
And an unpaid King's ransom
To try to work my way out of.
But at least I have a co-worker
And some minions, too.
We're bound to bear one another's burdens.

Earlier along the roadway
My path was smooth,
I was footloose,
And my hands were busy.
Like the fetters I now wear,
The manacles were my choice,
Because you have to hold your hands together
To catch your prodigal wages.
Turns out it's helpful for holding husks, too,
Not to mention clasping in prayer.

There was that brief epoch in which
I didn't belong to the Old Man
Nor yet to The Man,
And well before the Woman;
No manacles yet, first fetters off,
When I could have entered
The King's own refectory.
But, I hadn't learned yet to long for freedom,
And had already begun seeking slavery.
In the long run you give up the same things,
You just put them down sooner
Instead of carrying them with you
Until God takes your burdens off.

ON RENUNCIATION OF THE WORLD

21

Some people living carelessly in the world have asked me: 'We have wives and are beset with social cares, and how can we lead the solitary life?' I replied to them: 'Do all the good you can; do not speak evil of anyone; do not steal from anyone; do not lie to anyone; do not be arrogant towards anyone; do not hate any one; be sure you go to church; be compassionate to the needy; do not offend anyone; do not wreck another man's domestic happiness;[3] and be content with what your own wives can give you. If you behave in this way you will not be far from the Kingdom of Heaven.'

3 Lit. 'go near the bed of another'.

On Trochaic Feet
If You Think Monasticism Is Hard...

If you think monasticism is hard, holy crap!
Did he not hear me when I said I had a wife?
But still he leaves me with no viable excuse, dammit.
Suffocating between the bosoms and the bishop,
Just can't seem to get uncomfortable anywhere.
Thought I could get a release of some sort,
From matrimony or monasticism.

But here I am, stuck in the middle with you,
And with all my favorite vices denied!
Am I a man or a monk? I have no choice
But to man up, but man! I'd rather be a monk.
Refraining from evil is good, but it isn't doing good.
I'd say the Abbot had it out for me,
But if you don't have anything nice to say…
Say something nice anyway, and mean it.

I've always been a generous fellow,
Even with other people's things.
I only steal what I'm not going to keep.
I cannot tell a lie: I just cannot tell the whole truth.
Telling the truth takes humility, and I know
You can't handle the truth, and neither can I.

Truth is, I really hate those people
Down at the church, with their hands out
Wanting something all the time, like
My money, my time, my food, my hands,
Like we all belong to the same body.
It's bad enough to share a cup.

I thought I was supposed to love my neighbor
As myself, but my neighbor's husband objects,
And my wife's not too thrilled, either.
I guess that line of thinking wouldn't work
So well in a monastery, either - for most.
Might be better than what I'm getting at home.

Oh hell, I guess I've got farther to go to get
To Heaven than I thought I had.
Guess I'd better head to the prayer closet.

On Renunciation of the World

22

*L*et us charge into the good fight with joy and love without being afraid of our enemies. Though unseen themselves, they can look at the face of our soul, and if they see it altered by fear, they take up arms against us all the more fiercely. For the cunning creatures have observed that we are scared. So let us take up arms against them courageously. No one will fight with a resolute fighter.

On Trochaic Feet
YOUR DEMONS ALL KNOW YOU BY NAME

Your demons all know you by name
And they giggle with glee when you're scared
They'll attack ferociously
Til you're dead or you flee
So it's time for you to be prepared

Your demons all know you by name
They can see the fear in the eyes of your soul
So close your eyes and pray
And then go forth and slay
In the name of Him who makes you whole

Your demons all know you by name
And they tremble when you take up arms
If you screw up your nerve
And attack them with verve
Hell retreats with righteous alarms

Your demons all know you by name
So does the Lord of the Heavenly Host
Attack with joy in His name
Let your face with love flame
Rout the demons from pillar to post

ON RENUNCIATION OF THE WORLD

23

The Lord designedly makes easy the battles of beginners so that they should not immediately return to the world at the outset. And so rejoice in the Lord always, all servants of His, detecting in this the first sign of the Master's love for us, and a sign that He Himself has called us. But when God sees courageous souls, He has often been known to act in this way: He lets them have conflicts from the very beginning in order to crown them the sooner. But the Lord hides the difficulty[4] of this contest from those in the world. For if they were to know, no one would renounce the world.

4 Some texts add: 'or rather, the easiness'.

On Trochaic Feet
I WANT YOU WITH ME

Let me make it easy on ya
Let me take it easy on ya
I want you with me
Want to show how much I love ya
I don't want to have to shove ya
I want you with me

Won't you stay with me forever
Leave the world and go back never
What you gain's worth what you'll lose forevermore
I want you with me

Let me make it easy on ya
Let me take it easy on ya
I want you with me
Want to show how much I love ya
I don't want to have to shove ya
I want you with me

Sometimes we seem very distant
I'll help you to be persistent
So that we can be together constantly
I want you with me

Let me make it easy on ya
Let me take it easy on ya
I want you with me
Want to show how much I love ya
I don't want to have to shove ya
I want you with me

I want you to want me too
Easy does it if you do
You know I'll always wait for you to come
I want you with me

On Renunciation of the World

24

Offer to Christ the labours of your youth, and in your old age you will rejoice in the wealth of dispassion. What is gathered in youth nourishes and comforts those who are tired out in old age. In our youth let us labour ardently and let us run vigilantly, for the hour of death is unknown. We have very evil and dangerous, cunning, unscrupulous foes, who hold fire in their hands and try to burn the temple of God with the flame that is in it. These foes are strong; they never sleep; they are incorporeal and invisible. Let no one when he is young listen to his enemies, the demons, when they say to him: 'Do not wear out your flesh lest you make it sick and weak.' For you will scarcely find anyone, especially in the present generation, who is determined to mortify his flesh, although he might deprive himself of many pleasant dishes. The aim of this demon is to make the very outset of our spiritual life lax and negligent, and then make the end correspond to the beginning.

On Trochaic Feet
WORK

This is a note
To those of tomorrow
From us of yesterday:
There is a single creative Word
That should define your young life:
Work.
Take it from an old man
Hardened by lack of effort.
While the fire's burning in the furnace
Hammer out your horseshoes;
There's no such thing as luck,
But coming close counts as a viable option,
And better than hand grenades.
Work
Teaches you to control the fire
Instead of being consumed by it;
How to be a fire-break.
It's not just the fire inside -
Here there be dragons.
They're dangerous because
They want to teach you to play with fire.
Work
At things like fasting from flesh
So you can save your flesh from the fire.
Prostrate to make yourself a smaller target.
Pray or be preyed upon.
They will try to convince you that
Work
Will wear you down and make you sick,
And it might - it might kill you.
But not as fast as indulging the flesh.
That kills you while you're still alive;
Work
Makes you live after you are dead.
We go and work and God makes our meals.
It might be a lot of work for just bread and wine,
But it's the only way to build a body.

ON RENUNCIATION OF THE WORLD

25

Those who have really determined to serve Christ, with the help of spiritual fathers and their own self-knowledge will strive before all else to choose a place, and a way of life, and a habitation, and exercises suitable for them. For community life is not for all, on account of greed; and not for all are places of solitude, on account of anger. But each will consider what is most suited to his needs.

On Trochaic Feet
A PLACE PREPARED

Some need a place of solitude
To get their spiritual on
Some need stained glass windows
And a pipe organ
Some need the cathedral of the woods
Some need the wide and wet
Some need crowds and conversation
Some need nothing but net

Some sit enthroned on porcelain
Some prostrate on the floor
Some enter into their closet
Some must go out the door
Some read a book, some read the sky
Some read another's face
Some need a shoulder to cry on
Some just a virtual embrace

Some need the fathers that have passed
Some need the fathers here
All need the Father of us all
Thank God he's ever near
No matter what we need there is
A place prepared for us
A way to go and work to do
And we will meet him thus

ON RENUNCIATION OF THE WORLD

26

The whole monastic state consists of three specific kinds of establishment: either the retirement and solitude of a spiritual athlete, or living in silence with one or two others, or settling patiently in a community. Turn not to the right hand nor to the left,¹ but follow the King's highway.² Of the three ways of life stated above, the second is suitable for many people, for it is said: 'Woe unto him who is alone when he falleth' into despondency or lethargy or laziness or despair, 'and hath not another among men to lift him up'.³ 'For where two or three are gathered in My name, there am I in the midst of them,' said the Lord.⁴

1 Proverbs iv, 28. "They that forsake the law praise the wicked: but such as keep the law contend with them."
2 Numbers xx, 17. "Let us pass, I pray thee, through thy country: we will not pass through the fields, or through the vineyards, neither will we drink of the water of the wells: we will go by the king's high way, we will not turn to the right hand nor to the left, until we have passed thy borders."
3 Ecclesiastes iv, 10. "For if they fall, the one will lift up his fellow: but woe to him that is alone when he falleth; for he hath not another to help him up."
4 St. Matthew xviii, 20.

On Trochaic Feet
Solitude, Silence, or Settling

Solitude, silence, or settling
Most can't handle any one of those by itself
We talk on the phone
In the car
With the radio on
Ignoring the kids in the back seat

Isolation is not solitude
Deafening cacophony is not silence
Sitting still at 60 mph is not settling

Most go nuts in solitude
Unless they remember that
Alone is not loneliness
There's a Helper and His Host

If a person wants to go without
Breaking the silence
He must be broken first
So his mouth and mind can be still
While his heart cries out unceasingly

Settling patiently is unsettling
You have to stand and wait
Or bow and prostrate
Not sit and wait for fate

Practice all three in their proper place
We're all monks, going it alone
All together as one body

If we don't join the one
We really are alone
Without form, and void
Chaos and cacophony
Devoid of lifting spirit

Climbing The Ladder

On Trochaic Feet

Extras

Three is company, four's a crowd
But one is silence much too loud
Pray closeted or in the Church
But in your spiritual search
Take only those you hold by hand
One person who can help you stand
And God Who all your footsteps planned

~~~~~~~~

Life is one big buddy system, it has been from the start
When God took a rib out of the man and made another heart
It's not good to be alone or to get lost in the crowd
When two walk hand-in-hand with God the row is easily plowed

ON RENUNCIATION OF THE WORLD

27

So who is a faithful and wise monk? He who has kept his fervour unabated, and to the end of his life has not ceased daily to add fire to fire, fervour to fervour, zeal to zeal, love to love.[5]

This is the first step. Let him who has set foot on it not turn back.

[5] The order of these words varies in different MSS.

On Trochaic Feet
THE FIRST TRIP

The journey of a lifetime begins with the first trip
And fall over our own feet
One foot over-and-under the other
Until one gets a little balance in life
Which you get by holding the hand of somebody bigger

Life is a school-day quest to become a mathlete
Trying to get everything to add up
Preferably before we multiply
But we have to start with faith
Which sometimes seems like an imaginary number

We have to grow everything from seeds implanted
Except faith, which is given to us whole
Rooted in the ground of faith
And growing away from earth
Like a beanstalk climbing up a ladder heavenward

The paradox of a passion for passionlessness
Is like that of unselfish love
By loving another as yourself
Which is the only way love grows
Multiplying its fruit an hundredfold after its own kind

Climbing The Ladder

On Trochaic Feet
1. Up

WHATEVER YOU DO DON'T LOOK DOWN

Whatever you do, don't look down
You are not high enough yet
Earth is still close enough to touch
Just one small step for a man
But it seems like it's so much
The decision to leave the Earth
And reach Heaven if you can
Feels like a second birth
Through pain and blood and sweat
Formed from dust out of the ground

If it's like this at the bottom
What's it like when you get high
Where air is weak and gravity strong
Body yearning to feel the fall
When it seems you've climbed so long
With a lifetime still to go
And the ladder, the ladder is all
The only ground around you know
And Heaven is just a sigh
And Earth is brimstoned like Sodom

You could go back to your old ways
At your ease with your disease
And content with discontentment
Confront your demons where they thrive
Clinging only to resentment
Against a life you've never tried
But if you climb up you'll arrive
Safely on the other side
You'll fall down upon your knees
And cry grateful tears for grace

On Detachment

1

The man who really loves the Lord, who has made a real effort to find the coming Kingdom, who has really begun to be troubled by his sins, who is really mindful of eternal torment and judgment, who really lives in fear of his own departure, will not love, care or worry about money, or possessions, or parents, or worldly glory, or friends, or brothers, or anything at all on earth. But having shaken off all ties with earthly things and having stripped himself of all his cares, and having come to hate even his own flesh, and having stripped himself of everything, he will follow Christ without anxiety or hesitation, always looking heavenward and expecting help from there, according to the word of the holy man: *My soul sticks close behind Thee,*[6] and according to the ever-memorable author who said: *I have not wearied of following Thee, nor have I desired the day (or rest) of man, O Lord.*[7]

6 *Psalm lxii, 9. (R.V. Psalm lxiii, 8); 'My soul followeth hard after Thee'. Using the Old Latin, Agglutinata est anima mea post Te, my soul is glued behind Thee, St. Augustine asks: 'What is that glue? It is love.' And St. Chrysostom compares this close union to the nails of the Cross.*

7 *Jeremiah xvii, 16.*

On Trochaic Feet
OH HELL, I'VE GOT TO GO

Oh Hell, I've got to go
Can't wait to find a safe place to rest
Chased out by my past
Drawn out to run by a love that's best

There's nothing I won't leave behind
If that's the only way to find
A place where his love and mine
Can rest forevermore

Oh Hell, I've got to run
Running after him without resting
There's nothing but the goal
Cutting off the flesh protesting

There's nothing I won't leave behind
If that's the only way to find
A place where his love and mine
Can rest forevermore

Oh Hell, you've got to stay
If you're against me you can't be with me
Resting only on the nails
I'll reach Paradise where he'll be

There's nothing I won't leave behind
If that's the only way to find
A place where his love and mine
Can rest forevermore

ON DETACHMENT

2

*A*fter our call, which comes from God and not man, we have left all that is mentioned above, and it is a great disgrace for us to worry about anything that cannot help us in the hour of our need—that is to say, the hour of our death. For as the Lord said, this means looking back and not being fit for the Kingdom of Heaven.[8] Knowing how fickle we novices are and how easily we turn to the world through visiting, or being with, worldly people, when someone said to Him: 'Suffer me first to go and bury my father,' our Lord replied, 'Leave the dead to bury their own dead.'[9]

8 *St. Luke ix, 62.*
9 *St. Matthew viii, 22.*

On Trochaic Feet
Hangin' with the Zombies

Hangin' with the zombies
Trying to stay undead
There's no good death if life has been unlived
Don't want to put my folks down
But they should be in the ground
I'll wait around and hope I'm not outlived

Hangin' with the zombies
They just want me for my brain
I'm not using it while I am here
I used to capture thoughts, once
The way they've captured me
But I don't have to think if I just fear

Hangin' with the zombies
Don't know they're already dead
I often wish that I was just like them
And then there comes that hunger
To eat the flesh of God
If I don't then I will be condemned

Hangin' with the zombies
If I just had half a brain
I'd leave the dead to bury their own dead
Go back and join the body
The reanimated corpse
Who gives me his own flesh to eat instead

Hangin' with the zombies
Oh Lord, I've got to go
I feel the tug of death upon my soul
I've left my pound of flesh here
The rest belongs to God
Before I die I hope to be made whole

On Detachment

3

After our renunciation of the world, the demons suggest to us that we should envy those living in the world who are merciful and compassionate, and be sorry for ourselves as deprived of these virtues. The aim of our foes is, by false humility, either to make us return to the world, or, if we remain monks, to plunge us into despair. It is possible to belittle those living in the world out of conceit; and it is also possible to disparage them behind their backs in order to avoid despair and to obtain hope.

On Trochaic Feet
I Wonder What Hell Will Be Like

I wonder what Hell will be like
With all the good people going there
And people like me going up
Since pigs have wings after all.
How can they care so much,
Bastards without a Mother's love,
Without a Brother closer than a friend,
With only a prodigal Father?
How did they get all the tools,
And I got left in the tool box?
I bet Bill Gates would cup his hands
So Steve Jobs could drink first
If only there were water in Hell;
But I'd be hiding behind the Pearly Gates
Sipping from my own private puddle,
Hoarding apples as if the Millenium
Was beginning with a Y2K bang.
I have one thing they don't, though,
I've got God, the right God, my God,
Right here in my own little box.
And if you haven't got a box of God,
You haven't got anything, really.
I keep telling myself it's better
To have God than to be good.
These hellions are trying to be good;
I'm only trying to be God.

ON DETACHMENT

4

Let us listen to what the Lord said to the young man who had fulfilled nearly all the commandments: 'One thing thou lackest; sell what thou hast and give to the poor[1] and become a beggar who receives alms from others.'

[1] St. Mark x, 21.

On Trochaic Feet
All I Still Need is Nothing

All I still need is nothing to get everything I want
But nothing is playing hard to get
I thought it was washed away in the baptismal font
But it seems I've not seen nothing yet

And I think I could give up all that I have for him
If I didn't have to give it all to you

The poor are blessed with nothing and they give it all away
But I can't seem to keep it just for me
I used my talents wisely and received my righteous pay
Without it all I don't know who I'd be

And I think I could give up all that I have for him
If I didn't have to give it all to you

I could make a prophet if I sold everything I had
And showed you where nothing could be found
But only a turned profit is enough to make me glad
So I'll bury all my treasure in the ground

And I think I could give up all that I have for him
If I didn't have to give it all to you
And I could beg for nothing if there was some I could skim
So I'll be good for nothing left for you

ON DETACHMENT

5

*H*aving resolved to run our race with ardour and fervour, let us consider carefully how the Lord gave judgment concerning all living in the world, speaking of even those who are alive as 'dead', when He said to someone: Leave those in the world who are 'dead' to bury the dead in body.² His wealth did not in the least prevent the young man from being baptized. And so it is in vain that some say that the Lord commanded him to sell what he had for the sake of baptism. This³ is more than sufficient to give us the most firm assurance of the surpassing glory of our vow.

2 St. Matthew viii, 22.

3 I.e. the story of the rich young man.

On Trochaic Feet
EXTRA WEIGHT

I never go anywhere without a spare tire
I never know when I might eat again
I may look fat but I blame it on my attire
I'll put down the doughnut if you'll tell me when

When is it time to drop the extra weight I carry 'round
To go back to the bare necessities
The things I keep that pull me from the sky into the ground
Can I wait 'til they force me to my knees

I need to fill my head with facts and innuendo
The still small voice is too short a playlist
I've got to plug in and tune out when I am on the go
But I'll listen to you if you will insist

When is it time to drop the extra weight I carry 'round
To go back to the bare necessities
The things I keep that pull me from the sky into the ground
Can I wait 'til they force me to my knees

I cannot live unless that one is tied into my life
She pulls the strings that make my beating heart
Prying her from my arms would filet me like a knife
Until I let her go I will be torn apart

When is it time to drop the extra weight I carry 'round
To go back to the bare necessities
The things I keep that pull me from the sky into the ground
Can I wait 'til they force me to my knees

I can't buy salvation from the things that drag me down
Nothing is worth everything to me
So I'll be a beggar and I'll beg until I get a crown
That I'll give up, and then I will be free

Because it's time to drop the extra weight I carry 'round
To go back to the bare necessities
The things I keep that pull me from the sky into the ground
I can't wait 'til they force me to my knees

On Detachment

6

It is worth investigating why those who live in the world and spend their life in vigils, fasts, labours and hardships, when they withdraw from the world and begin the monastic life, as if at some trial or on the practising ground, no longer continue the discipline of their former spurious and sham asceticism. I have seen how in the world they planted many different plants of the virtues, which were watered by vainglory as by an underground sewage pipe, and were hoed by ostentation, and for manure were heaped with praise. But when transplanted to a desert soil, inaccessible to people of the world and so not manured with the foul-smelling water of vanity, they withered at once. For water-loving plants are not such as to produce fruit in hard and arid training fields.

On Trochaic Feet
DESERT FLOWER

The likes are all you're wanting
You're seeking out the shares
You can only do what's right
If you can see who cares
You take another selfie
The icon of Saint You
But take all the eyes away
You won't know what to do

You're rooted in a cesspool
A sewer of accolade
Struggling to get noticed
But always in the shade
The desert sun is waiting
The pools of water deep
You're only seen like Hagar
But your rewards you keep

Come blossom in the desert
Come drink the waters pure
Uproot from the rose garden
Eternal fruit procure
Don't be a plastic flower
On a perpetual grave
Bring life into the desert
And untold souls you'll save

On Detachment

7

The man who has come to hate the world has escaped sorrow. But he who has an attachment to anything visible is not yet delivered from grief. For how is it possible not to be sad at the loss of something we love? We need to have great vigilance in all things. But we must give our whole attention to this above everything else. I have seen many people in the world, who by reason of cares, worries, occupations and vigils, avoided the wild desires of their body. But after entering the monastic life, and in complete freedom from anxiety, they polluted themselves in a pitiful way by the disturbing demands of the body.

On Trochaic Feet
I'M TOO BUSY

I'm too busy to be good
Too busy to be good
Virtue just eludes me

I'm too busy to be bad
Too busy to be bad
But I'm not good
And I'm too busy to be wicked
Too busy to be wicked
For iniquity or sin

And I'm too busy for your party
Too busy for your party
No way you'll see me sin
I'm a saint, you know what I mean
And I do my little cross at the icon
Yeah at the icon at the icon yeah
I do my little cross at the icon

And I'm too busy for bad thoughts
Too busy for bad thoughts
I don't do my oughts
And I'm too busy for my prayer
Too busy for my prayer does God even care

I'm a saint, you know what I mean
And I do my little cross at the icon
Yeah at the icon at the icon yeah
I do my little cross at the icon

I'm too busy for my
Too busy for my
Too busy for my

I'm a saint, you know what I mean
And I do my little cross at the icon
Yeah at the icon at the icon yeah
I do my little cross at the icon

Continued

Climbing The Ladder

On Trochaic Feet

I'm too busy for the cross
Too busy for the cross
Hands too full for the cross
I'm too busy to be good
Too busy to be good
Virtue just eludes me

And I'm too busy for this song

~Apologies to Right Said Fred

On Detachment

8

*L*et us pay close attention to ourselves so that we are not deceived into thinking that we are following the strait and narrow way when in actual fact we are keeping to the wide and broad way. The following will show you what the narrow way means: mortification of the stomach, all-night standing, water in moderation, short rations of bread, the purifying draught of dishonour, sneers, derision, insults, the cutting out of one's own will, patience in annoyances, unmurmuring endurance of scorn, disregard of insults, and the habit, when wronged, of bearing it sturdily; when slandered, of not being indignant; when humiliated, not to be angry; when condemned, to be humble. Blessed are they who follow the way we have just described, for theirs is the Kingdom of Heaven.[4]

4. St. Matthew v, 3—12.

On Trochaic Feet
SPIRITUALIZING

Spiritualizing doesn't make us spiritual
Fasting does mean going without food
Standing doesn't mean paying attention
Humility doesn't mean not boasting
Bearing insults doesn't mean holding it in
Don't be meta when you should be physical

You can't get full without being empty
You can't get strong without making yourself weak
You can't be lifted up without falling down

The narrow way and the wide way are both ways of destruction
The wide way ends in destruction
On the narrow way you are destroyed every step
But it leads to reconstruction
If you can't read the signs you're not following close enough

You can't be right without being wronged
You can't be saved without being condemned
You can't live without being mortified

The Physician deals with the physical
Sinfulness is the fruit of overeating
Strength requires standing for something
All cutting criticism is constructive
Anything that's cut off is dead weight
The spirit is unwilling unless the flesh is weak

On Detachment

10

After our renunciation, when the demons inflame our hearts by reminding us of our parents and brethren, then let us arm ourselves against them with prayer, and let us inflame ourselves with the remembrance of the eternal fire, so that by reminding ourselves of this, we may quench the untimely fire of our heart.

On Trochaic Feet
AND THE FIRE

I think of you and it burns
It burns like Hell
And I cannot tell you what I have still
Inside of me that I have to kill
Capturing every thought
That's burning me

And the fire
It burns out the flesh that I have left
And the fire
Burns before the icon in the cleft
And the fire
And the fire
And the fire
Quenches me

I pray like Hell while it burns
To think of you
And enter that Consuming Fire
To become flame, body, soul entire
Flame from without
And not from me

And the fire
It burns out the flesh that I have left
And the fire
Burns before the icon in the cleft
And the fire
And the fire
And the fire
Quenches me

And the fire
It burns eternally
And the fire
Makes us one from three
And the fire
And the fire
And the fire
Quenches me

On Detachment

11

If anyone thinks he is without attachment to some object, but is grieved at its loss, then he is completely deceiving himself.

On Trochaic Feet
SO YOU'RE NOT GONE

I walked away
It wasn't
Anything you did
I had to go, I had to go
I left it all
Everything
Should've stayed with you
I had to go, I had to go

I thought I had lost you
But I still miss you
So you're not gone
So you're not gone
I thought I had lost you
But I still miss you
So you're not gone

It's so hard
When it all
Follows behind
You've got to go, I can't let go
It's hurting me
But I just
Can't seem to mind
You've got to go, I can't let go

I thought I had lost you
But I still miss you
So you're not gone
So you're not gone
I thought I had lost you
But I still miss you
So you're not gone

I look into the mirror and I see you by my side
I tell myself you're not there but my flesh won't be denied
I thought I had lost you but I still miss you and I cried
So you're not gone
So you're not gone
And I still miss you
So you're not gone

On Detachment

12

If young people who are prone to the desires of physical love and to luxurious ways wish to enter the monastic life, let them exercise themselves in all fasting and prayer, and persuade themselves to abstain from all luxury and vice, lest their last state be worse than the first.[1] This harbour provides safety, but also exposes one to danger. Those who sail the spiritual seas know this. But it is a pitiful sight to behold those who have survived perils at sea suffering shipwreck in harbour.

1. St. Matthew xii, 45.

On Trochaic Feet

OK WITH THE LIVING, A WRECK IN THE LIVING ROOM

They can't drag you to do drugs
You won't step on first base
Every single outfit you wear
Shows off your natural face
You pray at the McDonald's
Raise your hand in Sunday School
Nobody would suspect that
Alone you are a fool

You're ok out with the living,
But a wreck in the living room
On the outside you're an icon
On the inside you're a tomb

You only swear on Bibles
Hand raised, hand on your heart
Your lips are sweet as honey
And they rarely ever part
You're humble and you show it
With everything you don't
You should live with the angels
But you know you probably won't

You're ok out with the living,
But a wreck in the living room
On the outside you're an icon
On the inside you're a tomb
Your pure angelic body
Wraps up a dead man's bones
Your voice borrowed from an angel
Gravels with strumpet tones

You live with hope eternal
That God will stay your hand
That who you are when you're you
Will become what you can stand
You're not alone wherever
We're a cemetery lot
And God's the Undertaker
We're all part of His plot

Continued

Climbing The Ladder

On Trochaic Feet

You're ok out with the living,
But a wreck in the living room
On the outside you're an icon
On the inside you're a tomb
Perpetual care is needed
A return into the womb
Your parts knit back together
Into a temple, not a tomb

Climbing The Ladder

ON DETACHMENT

This is the second step. Let those who run the race imitate not Lot's wife but Lot himself, and flee.

On Trochaic Feet
WHEN I WAS FIVE I LOOKED DOWN

When I was five I looked down.
My feet were where my head should be
And my head where mine is now,
And that was high enough to
Stop looking up or looking out
And look down and in instead.
It's no wonder I was frightened:
I looked where Death and Hell hang out.
I stood stock still, like a post
In the crotch of a tree, suspended.
There is only one way to flee
When you have your foot stuck in a tree:
Holler like Hell for help: Our Mother
Who art in kitchen, hollered be Thy name.
She always comes when her Son calls.

I still climb, lugging fear along.
We innately know the ground is too firm
And our heads belong in the clouds,
Even if our head and feet together
Think they should pound rocks.
Those who believe everything is material
Still dream of exploring Space.
Fear can freeze you like deep space,
Stopped dead in the middle of nothing,
Like a salt-mound in the desert.
It can cause a drunken stupor,
It can cause ill-conceived ideas,
Fear's too closely-related children.
Still I miscarry fear as I climb,
Like the dead weight of a child.

How then to escape, when it looks
Like nothing's left, like nothing's right,
When behind is filled to the brim with stone
And all you have is the clothes off your back?
Be sober, be vigilant, be forthcoming,
Avoid sulfur, salt, sidelong looks, and sin.
If the wife won't come, go home to Mother.
There is always only one righteous,
So your Sodom must be stoned, and

Continued

Climbing The Ladder

On Trochaic Feet

You must strike out for the rock
On which you will be broken, the rock
That is higher than you can climb
And still be on the plain old earth.
So flee for your new lot in life,
Leaving even the best soil behind.

Climbing The Ladder On Trochaic Feet
NOTES

I don't really like the idea of writing notes about the poems; however, from my poem-reading experience, I like it when somebody tells me more about what the poet was thinking when he wrote the poem. I like to catch nuances that I missed, and feel like the poet and I have an understanding. So, I'll give what I like to get. I hope they enhance your enjoyment of this work.

+

PAGE 7: Apophatic Apology

Apophatic means describing something in terms of what it isn't.

"The project will not be televised" comes from Gil Scott-Heron's poem "The Revolution Will Not Be Televised". If you don't know Scott-Heron's work, you're missing out.

My best friend's best friend asked me one Sunday, "Why do you ask so many uestions?" I replied, "To find out stuff."

+

PAGE 9: Sycamore

Zacchaeus: Luke 19
Zacchaeus was the definitive biblical climber, the one we learn about first in our childhood. He had one reason for climbing - seeing Jesus was a necessity, and he was personally insufficient to see him without help. That tells us all we need to know about climbing.

Jacob's Ladder: Genesis 28
This tells us where to climb - God extended a ladder from Heaven for us to climb up on, Christ the Word.

Climbing The Ladder On Trochaic Feet
NOTES

PAGE 10: How Does One Begin to Climb a Ladder

Luke 14:26-33 Counting the cost.

You'll see quite a bit through this process about my acrophobia. It's been one of my defining features most of my life. I had a nice job with a painter at one point, and had to quit because I couldn't consistently do the high work - Sometime I could get something done 30 feet in the air on a walkboard on top of a stepladder on top of an extension, and sometimes I'd freeze up halfway up a 12-foot ladder. There are plenty of parallels to my spiritual life there...

There are a couple of evolution references here. Just for the record, I'm not an evolutionist. Nor am I a creationist. I'm a crucicreationinst: the universe was created by Christ on the cross, as he was "slain from the foundation of the world". Any references I have that sounds like evolutionism or creationism should be taken in their literal sence, which is literary.

"Covered in that which we stole". This is a reference to confession. After we make a confession, we kneel and the priest places the portion of his vestments called the stole on our head and pronounces the absolution.

"Footprints in the Sand" is my least-favorite trite Christianese poem. For me, when I look back at the sands of time and don't see two sets of footprints, there's one set and drag marks.

✢

Climbing The Ladder On Trochaic Feet
NOTES

PAGE 12: Isn't This a Book for Monastics?

Apparently I worte this poem on the Monday after the Sixth Sunday after Pentecost, since the reading that day is I Corinthians 7:24-35.

"Belay that thought!" A climbing reference, in case you missed it.

There are numerous stories about the help the desert saints (and others) received from wild animals.

I showed this book to a Jewish friend, and the first thing he saw when he flipped it open was "Is the Torah for goyim?" He was impressed.

There is a long-held theory that the Celts are the lost tribes of Israel. My last name O'Shaughnessy qualifies me as Irish, although it's about the only thing Irish I have left to me.

And yes, that's true even if you re-gift.

+

PAGE 15: Isn't This a Book for Monastics?

"It's best to begin with God"

If I recall correctly, I was thinking about how spiritual classics of the West often begin with somebody recounting a dream - most notably Pilgrim's Progress. That in conjunction with The Ladder requires starting with Jacob's dream.

There are a lot of fun (for me) references in here (e.g. "mass movement") that I will let you find yourself. Contact me if you want to know if a particular thing is a pun - it probably is.

Nice quote you can use if you want: "Going up and growing up: Both of them require heads in the clouds"

I can't bring myself to condemn those who have left

Climbing The Ladder On Trochaic Feet
NOTES

Christianity due to the incredible stupidity of some Christians.

+

PAGE 19: Go On and Grab a Sunbeam

"Carrying the day" obviously doesn't mean "full of win" in this context - it's what you'd be doing if you had grabbed a sunbeam.

"Be grateful that you've got one" and following is a reference to Romans 1.

Hide it under a bushel - NOT!

+

PAGE 23: The Ballad of the Monastery

There are several works by spiritual seekers of various ilks who have visited monasteries as part of their search. It is in this light that I have included all of these groups in this list.

"The Troubador, and his wife" is a reference to John Michael Talbot, founder of the Little Portion Monastery in Arkansas.

+

PAGE 25: Get Away!

"And that is for your best". If you 've lived a life in rejection of God's love, you's really HATE Heaven...

+

PAGE 27: Simon Says

There are several Simons in the Bible, none of whom are simple. Two of them figure into this poem: Simon Peter, and Simon Magus.

Stanza 1 - Yes, I know that was Jude and not Peter, but it

Climbing The Ladder On Trochaic Feet
NOTES

sounds like something he'd have said.

"Speak the Word and feel no shame" - Can you? Maybe you better examine yourself for some of the Magus.

+

PAGE 31: I Need an Angel

"Fondled bondage .... reptilian king" - references to Egypt, which the Israelites were in such a hurry to leave, until they started to miss it in the desert. Much of the rest is allusion to the Exodus story, with overnotes of Romans 1.

"City of forgotten dieties ... fifth column" - We've come into the Promised Land, but we aren't the only ones who have been here. There are those who were here before, and living among us seducing us, and we need the strength to fight.

"To God damn them all" - ultimately, we need our sins to be condemned and ripped away from us.

+

PAGE 35: Beat Down

"My mind is in every way unstable" - James 1:8

+

PAGE 39: Burn Like a Martyr

"Holy water burns" - not a vampire reference; talking about baptism here. Although Spike at the end of Buffy the Vampire slayer...

"And take from him his load" - Galatians 6:1-5

+

Climbing The Ladder On Trochaic Feet
NOTES

PAGE 41: Let's Go Out

The structure is from the Ladder: innocence, fasting, and temperance. The song is a play on babies as mentioned in the passage, and Baby as used in popular music (or at least the music that was popular before it was known as "oldies").

+

PAGE 43: Flap Like a Fool

"New wings" was the starting point for this one.

"For whom the bell never rings" - how can I write about angels and wings without an It's a Wonderful Life reference?

+

PAGE 45: When You've Lost

"No words to pray" - that's the definition of "lost".

+

PAGE 47: Running

"Gone through the mill": when we put our nose to the grindstone, it's usually on top of us crushing out our life.

+

PAGE 49: The Way to Holiness

"This allegorical word" - of course, I HAD to write an allegory to go with the passage!

"Wynken, Blynken, and Nod" - you should know that nursery rhyme already. If not, look it up.

"Hieromeerkat Timon" - this was after his Hakuna Matata youth.

Climbing The Ladder On Trochaic Feet
NOTES

"Brotherly love" - love is the gratest thing in the world - next to a nice MLT: mutton lettuce and tomato, especially when the mutton is nice and lean, and the tomato is ripe. They're so perky. I love that.

+

PAGE 53: Of Course God's Watching

"But I am running \ Away from something" - whenever we are tempted, we are tempted away, not toward.

+

PAGE 55: Enjoyable Pain

Each stanza builds in length, just like workouts do for those that practice them.

"And your body filled with fire" - Abba Lot went to see Abba Joseph and said to him, "Abba as far as I can I say my little office, I fast a little, I pray and meditate, I live in peace and as far as I can, I purify my thoughts. What else can I do?" then the old man stood up and stretched his hands towards heaven. His fingers became like ten lamps of fire and he said to him, "If you will, you can become all flame."
- From the Desert Fathers

+

PAGE 59: Don't Count Out

Stanza 1 - The Parable of the Guests
Stanza 2 - The Parable of the Good Seed
Stanza 4 - even the backslider has a chance of salvation

+

Page 61: Vows

Of note here is that the Eastern Orthodox wedding service

Climbing The Ladder On Trochaic Feet
NOTES

includes no vows. Marriage is not a contract between two consenting adults, it is a sacramental action of creation by God.

"Robe or crown" - baptism or marriage.

"To keep living that way" - mouths that only eat the Eucharist and repent. If we could live that way, we'd need nothing else.

"By having nothing all your own" - that's what we all need more of: nothing. It's hard to get, as we'll talk about later on.

"By paying your vows to the Lord \ In the presence of all His people" - Psalm 115:18, sung in nearly every Orthodox service.

+

PAGE 63: Bound

"Bound hand and foot" - marriage, for those who don't have it and may not have recognized the description...

"A co-worker \ And some minions, too" - wife and kids.

"Old Man .... The Man .... The Woman" - free from dad, not owned yet by the job, not yet married. Could've become a monk then - of course, very few fundamentalist Baptists become monks.

"Already begun seeking slavery" - looking for a career and a family.

"You give up the same things" - being a monk is a career and a marriage.

+

PAGE 66

This is one of the most well-known passages from The Ladder, since it gives a nice list of rules for the non-monk to follow.

Climbing The Ladder On Trochaic Feet
NOTES

PAGE 67: If You Think Monasticism is Hard...

"I'd rather be a monk" - the grass is always greener...

"Refraining from evil is good, but it isn't doing good." - the law of Christ is to do, not to not do. It's not a passive abstention, but an active participation. Hence the rest of the stanza.

"And neither can I" - and it goes downhill from there. But admitting you have a problem is the first step, right?

+

PAGE 67: Your Demons All Know You By Name

"Know you by name" - from the idea that one has power over someone if one knows someone's true name. We often name ourselves by our sins.

+

PAGE 69: I Want You With Me

There's a pun in here for my personal enjoyment.

"Let me make it easy on ya" - "My yoke is easy, and my burden is light." God wants us to climb up, and he helps by building our strength as we go.

+

PAGE 71: Work

I Corinthians 12:13: "For by one Spirit are we all baptized into one body, whether we be Jews or Gentiles, whether we be bond or free; and have been all made to drink into one Spirit."

Liturgy - the public work of the Church; see also "Bodybuilding"

+

Climbing The Ladder On Trochaic Feet
NOTES

PAGE 73: A Place Prepared

In order: Church, nature, boat, friends, sports, drunk, pious, biblically pious, nature again, studious, astrologous, social, co-dependant, internet social, traditional, familial.

+

PAGE 73: Solitude, Silence, or Settling

The idea here is very Sound of Silencey. We have developed habits of ignoring all noise, even what we ought to hear, being by ourselves in public, and settling into a routine where we're never still. Only in community can we hear what God is speaking to us in the silence of our hearts at rest.

+

PAGE 73: Extras

God always plans some companion for us - he places us in families. That means typically a spiritual father, and for domestic monastics, a spouse.

+

PAGE 79: The First Trip

Math is a lot like faith, to me: either you get it, or you don't, but either way you can't explain it. But it works regardless.

+

PAGE 81: Whatever You Do Don't Look Down

"Body yearning to feel the fall" - I assume I'm not the only one who gets the urge to "fall" when up high, right?

+

Climbing The Ladder On Trochaic Feet
NOTES

PAGE 83: Oh Hell, I've Got To Go

"Oh Hell" is both an epithet and a reason here.

"Resting only on the nails" - The crucified one, in order to be able to expand his lungs, had to pull himself up on the nails. If he rested on them instead, he couldn't breathe and would die.

+

PAGE 85: Hangin' With the Zombies

Stanza 1: Luke 9:59-60, "Let the dead bury their own dead"
Plus, I'm a big fan of the zombie stories.
Stanza 2: II Corinthians 10:5
Stanza 3: John 6:54

+

PAGE 87: I Wonder What Hell Will Be Like

"You haven't got anything" - a Princess Bride reference.

+

PAGE 89: All I Still Need is Nothing

Matthew 25:14-30

+

PAGE 91: Extra Weight

These are in order from easiest to get rid of to the hardest: actual weight and greediness, to information and noise, to relationships.

"Force me to my knees": a reference to prayer.

+

Climbing The Ladder On Trochaic Feet
NOTES

PAGE 93: Desert Flower

We are flowers that bloom only when watched and affirmed, unless we are fake ones. We need to learn to bloom in the desert.

"You're only seen like Hagar": Genesis 16:13, "Thou God seest me."

+

PAGE 95: I'm Too Busy

The last sentence of the portion from the Ladder reminded me of the original this song. I know the way I most easily avoid sin is by simply being to busy to bother. It is when I have time and good intentions that I fail most.

+

PAGE 99: Spiritualizing

So often we make our attempts at obedience sound succesful by dumbing them down or making excuses. Let's face it: we're failures. We have to start by accepting that, and not accepting it.

+

PAGE 101: And the Fire

Fighting fire with fire, literally.

+

PAGE 103: So You're Not Gone

Admittedly, detachment is where I'm stuck. This poem probably portrays my mental state better than any other here.

+

Climbing The Ladder On Trochaic Feet
NOTES

PAGE 105: OK with the Living, a Wreck in the Living Room

Our "safe place" is our most dangerous.

+

PAGE 109: When I was Five I Looked Down

This is an autobiographical poem. I attribute my acrophobia to this event when I bcame stuck in a tree and couldn't get myself free to get down. Makes climbing ladders difficult.

"Down and in .... Where Death and Hell hang out."

"Our Mother\ Who art in kitchen": I tried to develop this into a whole prayer later, but couldn't make it work.

"Like a salt mound in the desert": Lot's wife

"Ill-conceived ideas": James 1:2-16

"Go home to Mother": The Church.

"On which you will be broken": Matthew 21:44

"Lot in life .... best soil behind": A reference to Lot's choice when he and Abraham decided to settle down in the land.

Climbing The Ladder On Trochaic Feet

Climbing The Ladder
A LIITLE BIT ABOUT *The Ladder of Divine Ascent*

That St John Climacus (Latin for Holy John the Ladder Guy) wrote, upon request, *The Ladder Of Divine Ascent* is just about all we know about him. He was apparently born in the 6th or 7th century, and was a monk at what is now Saint Catherine's Monastery. He lived there or in the general vicinity the rest of his life, finishing out his days as abbot of the monastery. Another John, the abbot of the monastery Raithu on the Red Sea, wrote to St John and asked him to write a manual for monks.

To fill this request, St John wrote *The Ladder Of Divine Ascent*.
He used the image of Jacob's Ladder as his form. He divided the book into 30 chapters, or "steps" of the ladder. He begins with an exposition of the ascetic life, and how it should be approached and lived. Then follows the majority of the work, how to overcome vice and replace it with virtue. He closes the work with the 4 aims of the ascetic life: prayer, stillness, dispassion, and love.

The Ladder joins books like *The Imitation of Christ* and *Pilgrim's Progress* as the most beloved and widely-read spiritual works of Christendom.

St John Climacus' feast day is March 30, the day that my parish, St John of the Ladder Orthodox Church in America in Greenville, SC, was dedicated.

On Trochaic Feet
A LIITLE BIT ABOUT *Kenneth A O'Shaughnessy*

I started reading about 1973, when I was 3 years old. I finally learned to spell my name by typing it on my mother's manual portable Smith-Corona when I was 5. Within a couple of years, I progressed beyond my name to writing fiction based on my spelling words. I wrote about a completely fictional adventurer named Kenneth Irishman - I was obviously an inventive child.

I discovered poetry as a writing medium about the time I discovered puberty, and poetry was much preferred. I started by emulating the poetry I was most exposed to: gospel hymns. I've written poetry off and on ever since, especially a stint in college during which I wrote regularly to my girlfriend at the time, a decade or so ago when I wrote some songs with Johnny Larrabbee and the band Potter's Creed, and the present day (beginning in September 2012). For the past slightly over a year, I've been writing poetry nearly daily, and, including the contents of this book, have written as of this point someplace close to 500 poems during this time.

I grew up Baptist, as one might suspect from my early hymn-writing. I was received into the Eastern Orthodox Church in 2006, at St John of the Ladder OCA in Greenville, SC. This is my first trip through the book for which my parish and its patron saint are named.

www.ingramcontent.com/pod-product-compliance
Lightning Source LLC
Chambersburg PA
CBHW071517040426
42444CB00008B/1691